# *The Light Shines Through*

Rev. Neville Koch

To Darrah,

Hope you will be encouraged and blessed

Neville Koch

June 12, 2021

# Table of Contents

# Foreword

This collection of chronologically presented stories, capture the essence of God's activity in the life of His son, Neville. In typical "servant" fashion, Neville makes this about God's story, unfolding in and through him. Capturing His story over the span of three score years and ten is never easy but Neville manages to do just that with humility and a consistent deference to God's work in shaping and forming him as a man after God's own heart.

For those who know him for a particular season of his life, these narratives place those seasons into context, providing you with an overview of how God had prepared, molded and formed a mass of clay into a vessel of honor. The micro-narratives of Neville as son, brother, friend, husband, father and pastor are woven in a way that highlight a single theme: God's call on his life as declared in Jeremiah 1: 5 - *"Before I formed you in the womb I knew you, and before you were born I set you apart and appointed you a prophet to the nations".*

Neville has been and continues to be an inspiration and a gift to those of us who had the privilege of knowing him. A courageous and passionate leader, a man of integrity and exceptional humility, Neville has left an indelible mark in the lives of those he touched and the organizations he served.

I've had the privilege and honor of journeying with Neville throughout most of his adult life. Storms, fog, rain and sunshine: we walked, ran and sang our way through them all, witnessing God at work in our lives and in the countless others that God placed in our pathway. It gives me great pleasure in prefacing this narrative as a dear friend and one of his spiritual offspring.

Chris Pullenayegem

# Preface

Shakespeare said, "If music be the food of love, play on". I've never played a musical instrument, but music has played a major part in my life; in practicing God's presence, not only in good times but also in times when it seems like God is far away. He never is. His presence is as real to us in our valleys as it is on the mountain peaks – and many are the times when our darkest moments have been turned into vestibules of God's shining light.

We have a lot to learn and be inspired by the book of Psalms (Songs) which clearly reveals to us the place of music in our lives by way of a two-way conversation from God to his redeemed people and from us to Him.

After my retirement as a pastor, and as I began my ministry as a Hospice Chaplain (ministering to dying patients and their families), I never felt so out of my depth. In search of God's enabling, through prayer, he led me to a liberating truth in Psalm 119:130 "The entrance of your word gives light"

It is not MY word but GOD'S word that sheds light in the darkness. I've got to let go and let God do what only HE can do. I am an instrument, He is the healer! -As a result, the light shone through in countless moments and in amazing ways as I learned to trust no longer in human effort and skills and to let Jesus, the Light, shine through. I will share some amazing examples of this in the last chapter of this book; in my experiences as a Hospice Chaplain.

This book is not a biography but a story of how God revealed Himself in very special moments and situations in my life and ministry - when I (and others) needed Him most.

I share these moments and experiences with a prayer that you, the reader, will be encouraged and enlightened by the same light in perplexing times of your own; in times when you were at your wits end and you did not know what to say, what to do, or more importantly, what to expect when it seems like all hope is gone.

Hear God speaking to you in the words of a song I loved so very much when I was growing up, sung by Jo Stafford in the 1950's:

IT IS NO SECRET WHAT GOD CAN DO

*The chimes of time ring out the news*
*Another day is through*
*Someone slipped and fell*
*Was that someone you?*
*You may have longed for added strength*
*Your courage to renew*
*Do not be disheartened*
*For I have news for you*

*It is no secret what God can do*
*What He's done for others, He'll do for you,*
*With arms wide open, He'll pardon you*
*It is no secret what God can do*

*There is no night for in His light*
*You never walk alone*
*Always feel at home*
*Wherever you may roam*
*There is no power can conquer you*
*While God is on your side*
*Take Him at His promise*
*Don't run away and hide*

It is no secret what God can do. These words have been etched in my memory and in my heart and I trust they will enlighten and encourage you - as it did for me.

Be blessed!

# *Chapter 1*- Beginnings

Having been born in the beautiful tropical island of Sri Lanka (formally known as Ceylon) I count myself blessed to have grown up in a land where one could see the hand of God all around you; a land of astonishing beauty and splendor; a country rated among the top five tourist destinations in the world.

## EARLY YEARS:

I was an only son among three sisters and guess that's where my survivor skills come from. Jokes aside, we were a close-knit, loving family for which I am deeply thankful. With two kind and caring parents, our small, modest home was always open to visitors: relatives, friends and sometimes strangers who at some point (often in adverse circumstances) needed a place to stay. Our hearts and home were always open to those in need – enrichening us, not in monetary terms, but relationally (our first lessons in demonstrating the empathy of Christ).

My mother was an amazing cook and a "stay at home" mom. My father worked for nearly forty years with the Ceylon Government Railway as a locomotive engine driver. This explains my passion for trains – having enjoyed countless train rides (with my dad) and stay-overs in Railway bungalows, each of them set in the exquisite beauty of various parts of the country. These times with my dad, together with the influence of my mum played no small part in shaping my life and core values in my formative and later years.

FROM HOME TO SCHOOL (My life at Wesley College, Colombo 1951 to 1963)

Next to and alongside a Christ-centered home and environment was a Christ-centered school. I thank God for my parent's choice of Wesley College for my primary, secondary and tertiary education – an outstanding and affordable educational institution, situated barely two miles away from our home.

Wesley College was founded in 1874 by British Missionaries and the Methodist Church in Ceylon. With much passion and foresight, the founding fathers made it explicitly clear that this boy's school, while being Christian in character, was to be open to children of all faiths and ethnic groups – a place of learning that provided all its pupils an equal opportunity of discovering our life's end and faith's tenets in a safe and friendly environment – a place where we learned early, to play marbles and cricket together, to love and respect one another in the midst of our diversity.

Wesley's school motto is "Ora et Labora!" (Pray and Work) – A motto that soon became my own life's adage and a lesson I learned at a very early age. It taught me the place and preeminence of prayer in every area of life and gave me the key to discovering how God shines through when we have run out of all human skills, abilities, and resources.

At Wesley, we were blessed with highly devoted teachers who taught us more than what was found in text books. They were mentors. They taught us to "look above" and to "look to the end" (Latin: Respice finem)! The influence and impact these teachers and godly Principals had on me and my spiritual formation is immeasurable. I owe so much to them and thank God for them. They taught us to love one another, to see the image of God in every human being – regardless of social standing, race, color or creed; no matter how damaged or broken that image might be. There is a Savior!

## MUSIC AND MINISTERING:

In 1954 (in Fourth Grade) I was selected by our music teacher to sing as a boy Soprano in the school choir. I hadn't realized it then but this incident had a significant impact on the rest of my life: a blessing that has shaped my life and contributed to my spiritual growth in no small way. It made me feel special to sing with the well-known Wesley College Choir. Ever since then, I have sung in many choirs, duets, trios, quartets and worship teams – each one playing a significant part in my love for music, my walk with God, and in ministering through music and song.

To God, the giver of gifts, be all honor and glory!

# Chapter 2: My Spiritual Journey

I was blessed by parents who guided me by precept and example in the knowledge and love of Christ. At the age of three, they enrolled me in Sunday school at the Dutch Reformed Church, Regent Street, Colombo. I remember one of the earliest choruses I learned: "Jesus loves me this I know, for the Bible tells me so; little ones to him belong, they are weak but He is strong!" It is a chorus I have sung to many elderly patients as a Hospice Chaplain and it was a joy to witness the glow in their eyes – many of them joyfully joining in the singing - dementia not withstanding!  These words gave me a life -long sense of BELONGING to someone BIGGER than ourselves.

It was at Sunday school (and later at church) that I learned and believed that the Bible is God's inspired Word - authoritative and final in all matters of faith and life (doctrine and practice). I embraced God's Word as "a lamp unto my feet and a light unto my path" (Psalms 119, verse 105). By God's grace, these words determined the direction of the rest of my life. Throughout my boyhood, having yielded my life to the Lordship of Christ and through the study of God's Word, my faith grew stronger and deeper each day.

Then came the 1960's which was known as the turbulent sixties. Like most teenagers, I felt the turbulence and was swayed by its strong and gusty winds. I experienced what one may call "a crisis of faith" or "a rocking of the boat." It was a time of conflicting pulls, interests and affections; a time of bruised and broken relationships (with lots of self - doubt and self- depreciation). It was also a time of losing many close relatives and friends who emigrated to Australia and other destinations- a time of much grief and pain.

At the age of nineteen I decided to migrate to Australia along with a close first cousin. While getting ready to submit my papers, God providentially intervened. When my Pastor heard about my plans to emigrate he was very upset and challenged me to re-think, pray, and seriously seek God's will about it. "Is there something you are running away from?" he asked me. That hit me hard!  I promised him I would take a prayerful second look.

My heart was fixed on Australia.  Giving up my dream was not going to be easy. That night, I wrestled with God (like Jacob did) for nearly four hours on my knees. In my conversation with the Lord, I felt a strong confirmation of his call to pastoral ministry – the call I was running away from.  I knew this was my 'hound of heaven' moment (like the poem by Francis Thompson). I tried human reasoning and bargaining with God.  At the same time, I felt God's overwhelming presence. Then, around 2.30 AM the next morning on September 6, 1964 - with tears of joy falling down my cheeks and in an act of full surrender, I said those four most difficult words in the Lord's Prayer , 'Thy will be done."

That same morning, I called my first cousin and told him of my change of plans.  So, instead of going to Australia (as planned), I applied for entrance to the Dutch Reformed Church Bible Institute and Seminary in Sri Lanka.  I was accepted as a student in January, 1965, and graduated in May, 1969.  I was then ordained as a Minister of the Word and Sacraments (a Minister of the

Dutch Reformed Church in Sri Lanka) on August 27, 1969, one month before my 25h birthday.

So began a new chapter in my life!


SEMINARY AND BEYOND:

You might think that the journey from Seminary onward was easy and plain sailing. As you might have guessed, it didn't turn out that way. Have you ever thought of dropping out of school?  I did.  It happened towards the end of my first year in Seminary.

Someone said, "Life is not a hundred yard dash – it is a long distance race". That may be true but it is not the whole truth - for it does not mention the hurdles (big and small) along the way.  I was told that the very first year in Seminary would be the hardest – and so it was. You ask me why?  For two reasons:

1) *A radical life-change.* It meant making radical self-disciplinary choices, giving up much of the things I loved the most so that I would not get side-tracked or derailed along the way.  In my quiet times with the Lord, I heard the voice of Jesus say many times, "Do you love me more than these?"

2) *A tough work-load.*  In my first semester, due to pressing circumstances related to the availability of

teaching staff, I had a work load of 24 units - including the study of Hebrew and Greek languages concurrently. Adding to the drama, I was tending a youthful broken heart just before final exams.

Going back to Seminary each week (on Sunday nights or Monday mornings) became increasingly hard to do and I feared that I was headed for a breakdown. One Sunday morning I was feeling so down and drained, I wrote a letter of resignation- intending to mail it the next day. But, God intervened in a strange way that afternoon which deterred me from doing so.

It happened in a Cemetery of all places. At a funeral service, I was standing by the graveside of a close friend, when I felt an amazing, surreal, and overwhelming sense of God's presence. I felt completely enveloped by God's love - and a deep peace came over me. It was as if God was saying to me, "I AM WITH YOU"

As I left the Cemetery, there was a battle still raging within me so I decided to confide in my Pastor, Rev. John Van Ens about it. He was surprised to see me at his home around 6.30 PM that day. He read my letter of resignation and for about 10 minutes, there was silence. I could see tears falling down his cheeks. Then, he wiped away his tears and said "Son, it is your choice, but promise me one thing – go home and pray about this one more time. Then, go back to Seminary tomorrow morning and give it one more chance. If things get harder or more burdensome, go ahead with your plan. Either way, you will be in my thoughts and prayers." He then prayed with me and in parting he said, "Go in peace and may the God of peace go with you." It is what I needed to hear.

On Monday morning, I went back to Seminary as I promised. To my surprise, even though the work load had hardly changed, the burden felt lighter. It was as if a huge boulder had fallen off my shoulder. Once again, God came through! From there on, there was no turning back.

As to be expected, there were more hurdles ahead; dealing with discouragement, disappointments, unrealistic expectations, sleep deprivation, physical and mental fatigue, pressure of studies and examinations, meeting deadlines, researching and writing term papers (sometimes two term papers a semester), fighting temptation and loneliness to name a few. The biggest of course being discouragement - one of Satan's deadliest tools to get us out of the race and deter us from finishing the course. In fact, early in my first year at Seminary, a senior colleague told me that I would never last more than two years in ministry. I felt so discouraged that that very night, I got down on my knees and prayed "Lord, if it be your will, give me forty" - He did! Forty and more!

He was there at every hurdle to cheer me on!

## *Chapter 3*: God's light shining through our darkest moments (when tragedy strikes)

There comes a time in our lives when we come face to face with life-threatening situations. I remember my first such encounter at the age of seven when I was in danger of losing my three year old sister, Romaine, diagnosed with chronic nephritis. For me, it turned to be an early lesson in relinquishing all my cares on God- a God who is sovereign, almighty, merciful, and one who cares for us more than we can ever imagine.

My parents were told that one of my sister's kidneys was totally defunct and that the other one was 95 percent dysfunctional. She was admitted to a leading children's hospital in Colombo. In an apparent attempt to flush the dysfunctional kidney, her Pediatrician ordered that she drink multiple bottles of water a day. The result: her body bloated to the extent that her skin was a shiny yellow and looking as if her stomach would burst and her eye lids reduced to two tiny slits.

At this stage, this doctor informed my parents that there was nothing more he could do to save her life. He said, "take her home and keep her comfortable.' In other words, she is dying and all hope is gone. Not giving up hope, as one last option, my parents took my sister to a leading kidney specialist (a man of great faith). It didn't take long for this nephrologist to give them the news that, at this stage, there was nothing he could do for their child. His parting words were, "only faith and prayer remain." Disheartened but also encouraged by those words, that is the hope my parents held on to. Many a fervent prayer was offered by parents, family, Church family, and friends.

By this time, in order to save the life of his child, my dad had incurred a large monetary debt which made a huge dent in our family income which lasted for many years later. As you can tell, it was a difficult time for us, but our faithful God and Father shone through in many special and surprising ways, keeping always His promise to provide ALL our need!

A CHANCE MEETING? REALLY?

I believe that with God, nothing happens by random chance or accident. Read on...

Having used up his entitled leave of absence in the first four months of the year, my dad resumed his work. A few days later, he drove his train from the railway yard on to the platform of the Colombo Fort Railway Station. There, on the platform, the Station Master noticed the look on my father's face and cared enough to ask my dad why he looked so troubled. My dad told him, "My little daughter is dying of nephritis and there is nothing doctors could do"

It so happened that the Station Master told my dad about his own son who was dying of nephritis and was healed by a Naturopath (Herbal medicinal doctor) at a village about thirty miles north- east of Colombo where we lived. He said to my dad, "I recommend that you take your daughter to him".

With that, the Station Master waived his green flag and the train was on its way.

On his return from work the next day, my dad and mom decided with the help of a neighbor and at great risk, to take Romaine to the naturopath.

Having looked at my sister, the doctor told my parents that at this stage, he couldn't give them any promises or guarantee of healing but he would do his best – on the sole condition that they would do exactly what they were told to do. The doctor then prescribed a variety of herbal medications and gave them instructions on how they should be given. Then he said something out of the ordinary, "On your way back home, as you reach the town of Negombo, take your daughter to the nearest beach and bury her in the sea sand up to her neck for about forty five minutes"

Trusting God and taking his (the doctor's) word, my parents did exactly as they were told. Believe it or not – in a few weeks the one dysfunctional kidney started functioning again. My little sister was healed! Once more when we needed him most, GOD SHOWED UP!

My sister Romaine, now 71 years old, has been living with one kidney alone since the age of three.

As I write this story of how God came through, I am encouraged to see a wall plaque in front of me – a quote from Beth Moore's book, 'Audacious,' which validate and re-enforce what I have said so far in this chapter pointing to how God provides and works all things according to His sovereign plan.

On a morning in July, 1983, my wife Lorraine and I were on our way to pick up our daughter Nicola's birthday cake when we observed many buildings around us were up in flames.  Due to a known surge of growing ethnic violence and sensing imminent danger, we turned our vehicle around and made hasty retreat home. On our way, we saw vehicles being stopped and set on fire. Soon, there were angry mobs looting and burning homes and shops- smoke rising almost everywhere we looked. The tension was intense and palpable.

We found out that this was a reaction to the killing of 13 Sinhalese soldiers in the north of the country by a terrorist group who called themselves the Tamil tigers. These incidents marked the beginnings of a civil war that lasted over thirty years at an estimated cost of well over 100,000 lives.

Beyond the toll of human life with thousands more injured, the war polarized ethnic communities and spread seeds of dis-trust, hatred, and fear all round. Hardly anyone could escape the horrors of war (which included sleepless nights, horrific dreams and nightmares). We were traumatized by the dangers all around us, by what we saw and heard, and by the imminent risk to human life (including our own).

On the very first night of the outburst of riots, arson, and looting, we needed to provide (at our own risk) refuge for about forty persons, some of them having had their homes destroyed and others huddled in fear looking for a safe place for the night. Some of them were with infants, children, and pets. Our church hall was turned into a place of refuge and safety. These were tense moments indeed.

Years later, mid-morning on January 31, 1996, the scare hit closer to home when a suicide bomber drove a truck containing about 440 pounds of high explosives and detonated it opposite the KLM office where my wife Lorraine was working.

I could see the carnage all around on TV. For three hours, I did not know if she was dead or alive. By the grace of God, she survived with only minor injuries. To this day, she still experiences the terrible trauma of that fateful day, now, thanks to God, to a lesser degree.

A very close friend of ours, who worked in an adjacent building, was hit by shrapnel from the bomb resulting in the loss of hearing in one ear. He had a close call. When I visited him in hospital the next morning, his head was wrapped up with bandages covered with blood. The husband of another friend of ours didn't make it. Hundreds died and many more were inflicted with minor or life-threatening injuries. When people ask us how we came through such a long and brutal war, I say "by God's grace, presence, and strength alone!"

## Chapter 4: Early years of ministry and beyond

My first pastorate was the Dutch Reformed Church at Regent Street, Colombo (August 1969 to December 1974). Interestingly, this church was my 'spiritual home;' this is where I was nurtured in the faith. This is where I was baptized, attended Sunday school, and Youth Fellowship where I hold many precious memories.

At that time, twenty five years of age and needing no formal introduction to the congregation, this 'rookie' slipped into the role of pastor. It was like diving into the deep end of the pool - called now to shepherd the flock I was once part of; called to faithfully preach and teach God's Word to those I once looked up to; called to provide pastoral care and counsel (and a host of other responsibilities). Feeling out of my depth led me to get on my knees and seek wisdom and guidance from above.

My first two years were mostly smooth with a few rough and stormy patches. Those storms were due mainly to unrealistic expectations and differences of opinion on certain issues (my first important lessons on handling church conflict).

Along the way I had feelings of isolation and loneliness for want of a small, core group of people with whom I could share my joy and my pain, with whom I could bare my heart and pray, with whom I could share my struggles, my vision, my dreams.

After five and a half years I was transferred (as part of general ministerial transfers) to the Dutch Reformed Church, Dehiwela (1975 to 1980).

In between transfers, in moments of reflection and self-assessment, I asked myself what did I do right and what could I have done better? What lasting legacy did I leave behind?

My honest answer to the last question was 'not much.' So, as I transitioned from Regent Street to Dehiwela, I prayed much, asking the Lord to give me a core group of F- A- T people (Faithful, Available, Teachable) with the goal and outcome of making disciples.

Within three months God came through. He answered my prayers at a Dehiwela Youth Fellowship Executive Team Retreat at Lewella, Kandy (in the hill country). On the very first night of the retreat, while encircled in group prayer, the entire group deeply felt an overwhelming presence of Christ. In my gut, I knew this was the answer to my prayers.

Throughout the retreat we were all aware of a powerful presence and moving of the Spirit among us. At the end of the retreat we covenanted to go deeper with God and with each other. Propelled by this force from above, we made a solemn promise to meet weekly at 6.00 AM for one year for discipleship and leadership training. As leader of the group and with the advice and concurrence of an 'inner circle,' we planned and prepared training materials as we went along. Bonded by Christ and fanned by the Spirit, the excitement, joy and commitment of the group never slacked or wavered.  Half way through that year I could excitedly sense and see the transformational impact these sessions were having on the group. We never lost sight of our commitment and goal – making disciples for Christ.

It did not take long for others in the Denomination to observe the Spirit at work among us - as evidenced by the growth and potential of this emerging group. A few young leaders from surrounding churches joined us as we extended the duration of our weekly meetings for another year (now to be led by a new crop of leaders from within). Soon, we were invited by the larger body, the DRC Youth Federation to conduct the Leadership Training Program for future Youth Camps. By the grace of God, the fruit and effectiveness of this movement spread exponentially over the years and the church (local and national) reaped a harvest of Spirit filled, Spirit equipped, and Spirit empowered leaders. Praise to God from whom all blessings flow!

## CALVIN THEOLOGICAL SEMINARY

In August 1977, I left Sri Lanka to continue theological studies (a M.Div. program) at Calvin Theological Seminary in Grand Rapids, Michigan, USA. This M Div. program included a CPE component (Clinical Pastoral Education) which I did at Pinerest Christian (Psychiatric) Hospital in the summer of 1978. CPE is a hands-on clinical experience at an accredited hospital. Here at Pinerest, I worked in a ward with depressed patients. On the whole, this was an invaluable learning experience for me – further equipping me for pastoral care on my return to Sri Lanka.

On hindsight, I see that the Lord was prepping me to be a Hospice Chaplain here in the States. I found out 30 years later that the two qualifications for Hospice Chaplains nation-wide are a M.Div. and CPE! Talk about a God who goes ahead of us. Think about it, God in this instance was 30 years ahead of me at a time when I had absolutely no idea of emigrating ANYWHERE. Sovereign Lord, we worship and adore You!

On my return to Sri Lanka, these two programs equipped me in various and unimaginable ways - and opened more doors for ministry as I served in the Dutch Reformed Churches and the wider church, the body of Christ in Sri Lanka, in leading counseling and leadership seminars. Also, it equipped me to serve as Chairman of several evangelical agencies and organizations such as the Evangelical Alliance of Sri Lanka (EASL) and Lanka Evangelical Alliance Development Service (LEADS) as a founder member and first Chairman. And later, I served as the first Principal of the Colombo Theological Seminary, an Inter-Denominational Evangelical Theological Seminary founded in April 1994.

July 1983 saw the outbreak of the deadly civil war I talked about in chapter three and with that, winds of change. In the late 1980s and early 1990s, having being exposed to the brutalities of war and the depths of human suffering for so long, I became aware of a growing numbness to pain (as if my psyche could take no more) and I felt as if I was losing my shepherd's heart. I shared this confidentially with my discipleship group and requested their prayers. They were empathetic and supportive. After much prayer together and in discussions that followed, we were unanimous that may be, the Lord is calling me to a different area of ministry. Was it teaching? Was it counseling or discipleship training?

I went on to bare my heart before the Lord in soul-searching prayer. By the middle of 1990, still with no resolution and no clear leading from God, I decided, like Gideon, to 'put out a fleece' before him (the fleece thing had never worked for me before). So I said, "Lord, if it is your will for me to change tracks let it come completely from out of the blue (no job searching, no applications, no dropping hints, no sharing this with anyone). Let it be a total surprise. Then I would know, without a doubt, this is your leading!

Two years later, early in 1992, there was still no answer to my prayer. I was still waiting on the Lord. It so happened that, at this time I was Chairman of the Evangelical Alliance of Sri Lanka and for a long time (nearly three decades) EASL felt a need for an Inter-denominational Evangelical Theological Seminary in Colombo. Multiple attempts to make this a reality failed. By now the idea was on 'back burner" status. Then, something happened to resuscitate this long felt need. We (the EASL), received a letter from the Secretary of the Assemblies of God Bible School in Colombo saying that their Board was willing to dissolve itself and hand over the school completely to the EASL. The Board prayerfully accepted the offer and appointed an Interim Committee with a mandate to work towards "giving birth" to the Seminary we had been dreaming about and praying for – for so long.

I was voted as Chairman of the Interim Committee. The Interim Committee set a two-year time line for the work to be done. The core belief that motivated us to do the work we were called to do was, 'this is of God" - a belief confirmed by the Lord himself by the way he showed up in multiple situations along the way – things we could never have achieved without him. Yes, miracles.

The work of the Interim Committee was intensive and time consuming.

Guided by the Spirit, in two years, after much prayer and diligent work, Colombo Theological Seminary was ready to be launched.

Then the search for its first principal began. Initially, a few names were raised and discussed by the Interim Committee, but no decision was taken. The person I had in mind was currently living in Toronto, Canada – someone who, as far as we knew, was committed to returning to Sri Lanka to teach at the Colombo Bible College (now non- operational).

Then one day, the Vice Chairman and Secretary of the Interim Committee – Dr. Ajith Fernando and Pastor Eran Wickremaratne told me that they would like to meet with me sometime. I had no idea what this meeting was about. At this meeting they told me that they had been praying much about the appointing of a principal – and the Lord has been guiding them and the Interim Committee to ask me to fill that spot.

Instantly I had goose bumps as I remembered my prayer of two years ago. This certainly came totally out of the blue. This was to me, a word of affirmation from the Lord to change tracks; to step out in faith and out of my comfort zone into a new and challenging vocation; to a work I never dreamed of or never aspired to.

Having obtained release from my Church for two years, it finally dawned on me that God had answered my prayers in such a mysterious way. It took long – but then we know that God is always on time! This was for me a new beginning. I would soon see God at work in even more mysterious ways as CTS loosed the anchor and set sail into unknown waters in April 1994. Miracle after miracle kept re-assuring us (the board and staff) that this was and is indeed a work of God!

At the end of our second year at CTS we saw God at work in marvelous ways. CTS grew from around 20 students to 94 and we were soon running out of classroom space. Together, with the support and availability of several church leaders and teachers, CTS was able to consistently offer a total of six study courses per term, three terms a year, in three different languages (Sinhalese, Tamil and English). I am thrilled to hear that by the year 2016, the CTS student body had grown to an amazing 350 (inclusive of three satellite venues located around the country).

The year 1996 was a very eventful time for me and my family – marked by three very significant events. First, the explosion of the bomb on January 31st detonated opposite of my wife, Lorraine's work place and the trauma of that event (as shared earlier in chapter three). Second, the end of March marked the completion of my initial two year commitment as principal of CTS. I was pleased to be succeeded by two young, gifted and visionary leaders, Simon Fuller and Ivor Poobalan, who, I was confident, would be torch bearers of greater things to come. Third, also in March 1996, we (my family) received a letter from the US Embassy calling us for an interview with regard to our decision to emigrate. At the end of that interview we were informed that we had to make our first entry to the States by July 15, 1996. So on July 14, the four of us left Sri Lanka for the long journey (with 8 suitcases) to the United States and to another new beginning – with the conviction (after much prayer) that this is where the Lord was leading us as a family. A plunge into the unknown – knowing only that God will be our shepherd and guide every step of the way.

## Chapter 5: Another New Beginning (Life in America)

Our first year in the United States was full of challenges and surprises as we adapted to our new situation. It wasn't easy leaving the land of our birth, our family, our friends, our support systems, our churches, our jobs, and our schools for an unknown future and relative obscurity. God knew and felt our tears. Providentially, Nicola and Graeme didn't take long to gain entrance into good Christian schools. Nicola, having successfully done her SAT exam in Colombo in June 1996, went straight into College and Graeme into Year 7 or Junior High. What amazed us was how God shone through, providing us with finances for schooling at a time we could hardly afford it. It reminded us of Jehovah-jireh ,"God will provide" That could read, "God will find a way! Or, literally, "God will see to it" Praise God, he did!

We were also amazed at the smooth transitions and the new friends they made – just the right kind of supportive friends they needed at this stage of their lives. Nothing happened by chance or by accident. It was all by the providence of God.

I remembered something I memorized in the Heidelberg Catechism when I was in my teens (a long time ago):

Heidelberg Catechism Q & A 27; What is providence?

Providence is the almighty and ever present
power of God
By which he holds, as with his hand,
Heaven and earth and all creatures
And so rules over them that leaf and blade,
Rain and drought, fruitful and lean years,
Food and drink, health and sickness,
Prosperity and poverty – all things, in fact,
Come to us not by chance
But from his fatherly hand.

## A TESTIMONY TO HOW GREAT IS OUR GOD!

When we first arrived in the States, Lorraine's brother and his wife (who sponsored us and initially opened their home to us), advised us to purchase adequate health insurance for our family as a top priority. "Without it, they said, you could be in big trouble".

We called for quotes from several Insurance Companies and the minimum premium quoted was $ 600 per month – nowhere near what we could afford. So we got down on our knees and prayed, "Lord, be our Insurance, we are trusting in you."

Being "covered" by the Lord, our constant and never failing Insurance, in our first year here in the States, not one of us missed a day at school or at work, not one of us got sick. We didn't even know a doctor. God is faithful to His promises!

After four months, Lorraine found her first job through a 'Temp' agency, which led to greater job opportunities in the years ahead. At that time I felt God calling me back to pastoral ministry so I began the process of being declared "Eligible for Call" to the ministry in the Christian Reformed Church in North America – sending out letters, resumes and my bio data to several vacant churches in the denomination. Before long I realized that this process was going to take much longer than I expected – possibly even a year or longer! So, "to keep bread on the table" I started working at a factory on minimum wage.

My factory job helped in no small way to steady the boat, pay our bills and keep afloat. It also helped preparing me for the American way of life. For one year, during those eight hour days I made new and supportive friends (they all came for my Installation service – non-Christians and atheists included). While assembling 'Easy Reachers' (what you see being used to pick up trash on roads and freeways) I listened to the radio (with head phones) tuned into some great, inspiring Christian programs – feeding on God's Word and being refreshed in spirit by hymns and spiritual songs (old and new). It seemed as if the Lord was re-charging my batteries and preparing me (humbling me) for ministry ahead.

The search for a pastorate was long, intense, thorough and challenging but also invigorating. After a couple of disappointments and 'near calls,' I received a Call to Pastoral ministry from the Christian Reformed Church in San Diego.

The Rev. John Van Ens (my former pastor in Sri Lanka who encouraged me to go back to seminary when I wanted to quit as a student) was invited from Florida to preach God's Word at my Ordination/Installation Service on December 07, 1997.

Our time with Pastor John was very special as we reminisced on the past.

My family and I were deeply blessed with a caring, appreciative and supportive church family; with a spacious, beautiful parsonage and stable financial support. I retired on my 65th birthday, September 26, 2009- after a total of 40 years of pastoral ministry. All by grace alone!

As the date of my retirement drew near and sensing that the Lord was calling me to a new field of ministry, I began to prayerfully search for God's leading. My wife Lorraine suggested that we search the Internet for openings as a Volunteer Hospice Chaplain. We did and we found two hospice agencies in San Diego County with openings. We connected with them and soon I had calls and offers from both of them. I signed up with these agencies and enrolled for their Orientation programs. They were great learning experiences, inclusive of hospice visits under the supervision of Hospice RNs and Case Managers.

Barely two weeks later, to my surprise, the Director of Operations of one of them called me on the phone and asked me if I would be interested in joining them full time. Before she hung up she told me to think about it and let her know. When she ended the call, I bowed my head in prayer and thanked the Lord for this open door. So three weeks after retirement, mid October 2009, I commenced my work as a full time Hospice Chaplain. Another new beginning! For the occasion, I used as my prayer the words of a hymn from my old school Hymn book, "Lord, in the strength of grace, with a glad heart and free; myself, my residue of days, I consecrate to Thee"

I thank God for six more years of ministry, this time among dying patients and their grieving loved ones; all in need of pastoral care, of hope and comfort from above. There to hold the hand of someone breathing their last; to weep with those who weep; to stand beside families as they say their final good byes (letting go is hard to do).

In my role as Director of Bereavement Services, it was also my task to follow through with those left behind - to be in touch with them (for at least one year) and to assist them in the grieving process.

Many have asked me, "How do you do it?" I say: "It's a calling – and whoever God calls, he ENABLES and EMPOWERS." God's grace knows no bounds, His love knows no end!

## *Chapter 6*: My Hospice Experience

Let me start from the very beginning by responding to the question: what is the difference between hospital and hospice? A hospital provides a patient *curative* care whereas a hospice provides *palliative* care. The focus and goals are different. *Curative* provides healing and *palliative* provides comfort (when no healing is deemed possible). The criterion to qualify for hospice care is someone with a certified prognosis of six months or less to live. It is an end of life situation.

When I began my work as a hospice chaplain (after 40 years of pastoral ministry) I felt strangely inadequate at times (such as a first visit to a forty year old person who has just been told by his physician that he has only three months or less to live). Where do I begin? What do I say? I figured it was God's way of saying, "Trust in me, I will lead you on". It was also a timely reminder that our adequacy/sufficiency is in Christ alone.

It taught me to pray fervently before each visit that the Lord would reveal himself to me, my patients and their families" in his own surprising ways." It taught me to "let go and let God in." I learned that when God shows up there is hope - and something beyond us happens. Miracles of love and grace!

What follows are real life stories that demonstrate what I have said so far in this chapter. Note well: with the exception of Example Number One, actual names are withheld for privacy reasons.

Recently, when I visited Carlos Sotero at his residence, Carlos shared his own story of his experience of a miracle and said that his two daughters and son did not believe him. In fact, his son told him he must have been drunk. Carlos told them "I have a witness – he is Chaplain Neville" I told Carlos about the book I am writing and that it includes his story but not his actual name. He insisted however, that I include his name because he wants others to hear his testimony of what happened that day.

EXAMPLE NUMBER ONE:

Carlos Sotero is a Korean War Veteran of Italian descent. His wife, Rose, came under our (hospice) care with a diagnosis of end stage Alzheimer's. Rose and Carlos were happily married for 57 years. They lived together at a seniors facility – he, on the third floor; she, on the second floor (a floor set apart and secured for dementia patients).

Carlos loved Rose very dearly. He would spend an average of five to six hours daily beside Rose (caring for her). The problem was that she did not know him anymore. She appeared to be living in a faraway place and whenever I visited them, he would tell me, with tears, "This is not my Rose!"

Having heard that lament so often, my heart ached for him and for her. One day, on my way to see them, I prayed "Lord, please, please, please give Carlos and Rose one moment with you and with each other."

That day, both Carlos and I observed something different. Rose was propped up in her Lazy- boy wheel chair as usual – but as we (Carlos and I) were conversing together, it appeared as if Rose was listening to us (when usually she seemed to be oblivious to our presence). Towards the end of my visit I read Psalm 121: "I will lift up my eyes to the hills. Where does our help come from? Our help comes from the LORD, the maker of heaven and earth". I paused at that point to share a comforting word based on the text of scripture with Carlos (and with Rose if she was listening). Psalm

121: 3-8 gives us many assurances of God's constant care and safe keeping over us.

After a reading of the scriptures (Psalm 121), a parting prayer and a blessing, it was time to leave. I got up from my chair, placed my hand on Rose's shoulder and said to her, "Rose, never forget God is watching over you both now and forever more!" To our absolute amazement, this lady who had not spoken for several months said, "I know that".

I can still picture it vividly- in sheer excitement, Carlos jumped out of his chair, put his arms around her, kissed her and said, "Honey, I love you!" Rose smiled and said, "I love you too!" What an ecstatic, special moment – by the power of God's Word!

One week later, Rose went home to her permanent rest. As Carlos put it, "she got her wings" (it was hard but he was now ready to let her go). No more Alzheimer's, no more death, no more sorrow and no more pain. The light shone through in its brilliance. Miracles do happen!

EXAMPLE NUMBER TWO: Enid was in her late eighties. She was diagnosed with end stage (age- related)

Dementia. She hardly spoke a word. She was cared for by the only surviving member of the family, her son. She was 'a live wire' at her church. That was a long time ago. Now she was almost in a vegetative state – curled up in bed most of the time, waiting for God to call her home.

Then one day, at a Hospice Inter Disciplinary Group team meeting, one of the Registered Nurses reported that she (the patient) appeared to be dreadfully fearful of dying. Following a brief discussion by the team, I was asked to go and help calm her fears. On my regular bi-weekly visits, Enid hardly recognized me or acknowledged my presence. So I thought about how I was going to connect with her. I prayed, "Lord, I feel so helpless. How can I get through that wall (her dementia, her far away-ness)" I said, "I don't know, Lord, but I know YOU can!"

By the time I reached Enid's home I had a plan: Read/quote the scriptures- sing hymns of assurance and leave the rest in higher and more capable hands.

I was greeted at the door by Enid's son who then led the way to his mom's room. What I saw as I entered surprised me: the patient was (as usual) in bed- but this time in a position as if she was expecting or waiting for someone! I whispered a quick "Thank you Lord!" Enid greeted me with a smile for the very first time since I started visiting her four months ago. She said, "I was expecting you, thank you for coming."

I asked her if she would like me to read the scriptures and sing some hymns. She said, "Please do." So I read and quoted assuring scriptures, interspersing them with well- known hymns of faith, but each time I paused to ask, "Do you believe this?" she, with a feeble voice, replied, "I forget!" She kept saying the same thing – I forget!

After a while I felt as if there was a wall between us (a barrier). Was it demonic, dementia or something else? I felt a need to pray, so I whispered a prayer "Lord, whatever this wall may be, break it down in the power and authority of Your name, the Name above all names!" At the end of my prayer, I felt the Lord guiding me to read the Gospel of St. John, Chapter 11 (The raising of Lazarus from the dead and the conversation between Jesus and Martha).

I read John 11: verses 17 to 26

*17* *On his arrival, Jesus found that Lazarus had already been in the tomb for four days.*

*18* *Now Bethany was less than two miles[a] from Jerusalem,*

*19* *and many Jews had come to Martha and Mary to comfort them in the loss of their brother.*

*20* *When Martha heard that Jesus was coming, she went out to meet him, but Mary stayed at home.*

*21* *"Lord," Martha said to Jesus, "if you had been here, my brother would not have died.*

*22* *But I know that even now God will give you whatever you ask."*

*23* *Jesus said to her, "Your brother will rise again."*

*24* *Martha answered, "I know he will rise again in the resurrection at the last day."*

*25* *Jesus said to her, "I am the resurrection and the life. He who believes in me will live, even though he dies;*

*26* *and whoever lives and believes in me will never die. Do you believe this?"*

As soon as I read those last words, Enid smiled and said, "Yes, I believe". I had goose-bumps. With tears of joy, I asked Enid one final question: "Are you ready to go home?" With eyes all aglow she said "Yes, I am!"

In the verses that follow our scripture reading in John Chapter 11, we are told that when Jesus went to the tomb of his friend Lazarus, he said, "Lazarus, come out," and the dead man came out ALIVE!

Before I left that day Enid requested the sacrament of 'Holy Communion' on my next visit. We did celebrate the Lord's Supper together as planned. It was a foretaste of heaven. A couple of weeks later Enid went to where her soul was longing to go. The Light shone through!

EXAMPLE NUMBER THREE:

Her name is Sarah. On my first visit with her she made it very clear that she is Unitarian. Unitarians believe in God. They do not believe in the deity of Christ and in the Holy Trinity. She went on to say that she is not a practicing Unitarian – but Unitarian she will be till the end. As a matter of protocol, I assured her that I respect her beliefs and that I will be open to conversations related to spiritual matters if or when she feels free to talk about them. She, a very friendly lady, thanked me for my assurance and openness. Then she told me that on my regular visits she would like to know more about "Jesus, the man." She also asked me to pray, to read the scriptures and to sing some of her favorite hymns (she told me that the RN had told her I had a good voice). She called me Pastor.

Sarah was diagnosed with end stage Cardiac Disease. She was 67 years old and weighed less than 90 pounds. She was 80 percent blind (she could see me only as a shadow). She also suffered from an inoperable broken spine (by a fall) which caused her constant and excruciating pain. But she never complained and was often able to engage in interesting and invigorating conversations.

She wanted to die and had suicidal ideations. In fact, one day she asked me to assist her in committing suicide.

On my regular visits Sarah would ask questions about God, about my views of Jesus, of death and dying and life after death. She evidenced a searching heart and openness to new insights about Jesus. Then one day she said she had a very high view of Jesus – but she would NEVER (capitalized for emphasis) believe in Jesus – that Son of God stuff! She took me by surprise and I must confess I was deeply hurt inside. My heart was yearning for her to come to a saving knowledge of the truth. I whispered a prayer to Jesus: "Please Lord, reveal Yourself to her!"

After a while (and it was my time to leave) she told me to sing a hymn and pray before I left. I asked her if there was any particular hymn she would like me to sing? She said, "How Great Thou Art!" So I sang with affection:

*O Lord, my God, when I in awesome wonder*
*Consider all the works thy hands have made;*
*I see the stars, I hear the rolling thunder*
*Thy power throughout the universe displayed;*
*Then sings my soul, my Savior God to thee*
*How great thou art, how great thou art!*

*And when I think that God, his son not sparing,*
*Sent him to die, I scarce can take it in*

*That on the cross, my burden gladly bearing,*

*He bled and died to take away my sin.*

*Then sings my soul, my Savior God to thee*

*How great thou art, how great thou art!*

*When Christ shall come with shout of acclamation*

*And take me home, what joy shall fill my heart,*

*Then I shall bow in humble adoration*

*And there proclaim, my God, how great thou art!*

*Then sings my soul, my Savior God to thee*

*How great thou art, how great thou art!*

When I was done singing, I observed there were tears rolling down Sarah's cheeks. I didn't say a word – and neither did she. After minutes of silence I placed my hand on her shoulder and said, "God willing, I'll see you again next week."

One week later, as I arrived and before I said a word, Sarah said to me, "Pastor, I have something to tell you – last week as you were singing that song I saw a bright light on your face, I knew who it was!" That day she professed her faith in Jesus as her Savior. AMEN!!!

A couple of weeks later, Sarah moved on peacefully to that place in God's presence where there is no more death, no more sorrow and (mostly for her) NO MORE PAIN.

EXAMPLE NUMBER FOUR:

He once fought in the German army on the Russian front in World War II. Now he is terminally ill with Parkinson's disease. As he came under hospice care he could hardly talk anymore. He appeared to be deeply traumatized – having been shot four times by Russian fire and by the rigors of war. He seemed agitated by disturbing voices within him – and guilt laden for things he did and did not do.

The family identified him as "German Lutheran" but lost his way, having drifted from the faith of his fathers. I perceived that his greatest needs (in these last few weeks or months of his life) were inner healing, peace with God, deliverance from his inner 'demons,' freedom from guilt and fear; self- forgiveness and God's forgiveness. Let's call him Johannes and his wife, Jane.

Johannes and Jane were both feeling lost and helpless – gripped by a sense of hopelessness. I dealt with my own feelings of helplessness with questions like where do I begin? How do I proceed in penetrating the darkness? I started on my knees, confessing my own feelings of inadequacy - and handing over the reins to the One who can do (as the scriptures say) 'immeasurably more than we can ask or imagine!" Counting on God to penetrate the darkness, on my weekly visits I read relevant scriptures and offered prayers for deliverance. I also facilitated conversations among the three of us – enabling Johannes to connect the dots of his past and present.

I called it "afternoons with the Mulders!" – Every week, we sat around a table and was served by our host with chocolates, home-made cookies and a cup of "Ceylon Tea". Jane also provided family albums as helpful visual aids to stimulate her husband's memory of his family and military past. Slowly, they were beginning to see the light.

This was verbalized by Jane in a "Thank You card" I received into our 12th week together and I quote her opening sentence: "Dear Chaplain, thank you for giving us a perspective of what is left of the rest of our lives" By the grace of God, this also facilitated their "return to the faith" and basking in the sunshine of God's forgiving love!.

There came a time when Johannes knew for the first time what it is to be accepted and loved by God unconditionally, what it is to be forgiven and to be made' as white as snow' in God's eyes, through our Lord Jesus Christ. He was at peace with God as the Light shone through.

One Maundy Thursday afternoon (the day before Good Friday) Johannes was deemed to be "imminent" (in hospice language that means the patient is near and actively dying); body organs were shutting down and the patient could die at any moment). Johannes was now confined to his bed, in and out of consciousness, surrounded by his family – his dog sleeping by his side (refusing to eat or move as if he knew).

The family appeared to be at peace, exuding an aura of victory over death and the grave. So I sang two resurrection hymns: Charles Wesley's "Christ the Lord is Risen Today" and Robert Lowry's "Christ Arose" While I sang, both Jane and I observed Johannes relaxing and a slight smile on his face as if he was listening and responding, as if he was at peace and ready to go home. Holding his hand, I offered prayers for him and his family. I said what I knew was going to be my last and tearful goodbye to this incredible man.

The next day, on Good Friday evening, my wife Lorraine and I were at a "Tenebrae Service" at a Presbyterian Church downtown San Diego. The service was due to begin at 7:00 PM. Seated inside the church at 6:45 I felt my cell phone buzzing. I whispered to Lorraine, "I am sure that is Jane calling". When the service was over I checked my voicemail and so it was. It was Jane calling to say "Johannes is safely home".

EXAMPLE NUMBER FIVE:

Ronald was forty six years old when he was diagnosed with end stage Pulmonary Disease (COPD). He was told by his doctor that he had only three months to live. The news hit him like a bolt of lightning. That is when he came under hospice care. When I first visited him in his apartment (where he lived alone) his mother and brother had just heard the shocking news and were visiting him too. Ronald, shocked by his prognosis, was falling apart – rocking up and down on his chair as if he was in a trance. He was unresponsive. There was fear in his eyes and the only conversation I had that afternoon was with his family who shared some things about Ronald's past.

They said that Ronald had invited Jesus into his heart when he was fourteen years old. At sixteen, he manifested serious emotional and mental problems. He was diagnosed with Schizophrenia. Soon deviant and abusive behavior had caused a rift between him and his family (especially with his mother). Ronald left home and ended up living among drug addicts and prostitutes for nearly twenty five years.

Together with the Hospice Social Worker (who joined us half way through my visit), we discussed options for a workable 'Plan of Care'. Ronald's brother, John – the only family member who had kept in touch with him during his self-exile assured us of his own input and support in providing Ronald the kind of care he needed.

Driving home that evening I was at my wits end, with lots of unanswerable questions going through my mind. Will he remember me? Will he accept me and open up to me? Will he be calm or belligerent? That night and all through the week I spent much time in prayer seeking the empathy and wisdom I needed to "get a connection" with Ronald and how to move on in making a difference in restoring him to God's shalom.

A break- through came my way when I received a call from Ronald's brother two days before my second scheduled visit. We discussed a couple of approaches and options. At the end of our phone conversation, John told me that he was taking two weeks leave of absence from his job to enable him to spend more time "one on one" with his brother. Finally, he asked me to "covenant with him" in praying for Ronald's return to the Lord. I said to him, "count me in." So we became partners in prayer. The result was overwhelming as the Light shone through.

As I walked into Ronald's apartment on my second visit, I could tell that his brother had been with him. There was a change in his demeanor. He looked calm and rested. He appeared to be accepting of me and of the hospice team and our interventions.

It appeared he still had a long way to go in accepting his prognosis, dealing with guilt and shame and his fear of dying.

On a subsequent visit, believing that the entrance of God's word gives light and is powerful and sharper than any two edged sword, I read relevant scriptures on the subject of God's acceptance and forgiveness (from Psalms 32 and 51; Luke 15 (the story of the prodigal son); I John 1:9, trusting the Holy Spirit to penetrate the darkness in the light of God's LIBERATING LOVE.

Through use of the scriptures, God shone through – assuring Ronald of the Father's embracing, lavish and unconditional love. At the end of this visit, I was led to sing Amazing Grace. When I was done, Ronald smiled and said, "That's my song!"

He died four weeks later. That same evening his family and I were gathered around Ronald's bed. He was not talking anymore. Even with the use of oxygen, his breathing was getting slower and more labored. He appeared to be at peace and seemed to be aware of our presence. At one point I called the family aside and shared my view that Ronald would not make it through the night and now was the time to say their last goodbyes.

We gathered around Ronald's bed again. We said our last goodbyes. I read a few re-assuring scriptures, offered prayers and a parting blessing. It was a solemn, poignant healing moment. What was most moving was what followed at the end – a mother's kiss and a mother's prayer.

I left the apartment around 6.00 PM. I had hardly gone three miles when my cell phone rang. It was John, to say, "Ronald is safely home."

I was asked by the family to officiate at Ronald's memorial service, a service I will never forget. My message was titled "Going Home." I could tell that among those present, there were some who had doubts about Ronald's final destination. Based on what I knew about him in the past few weeks - his confession of sin, his repentant heart and his joy of forgiveness, I had no doubt about it. At the end of my message (to re-assure anyone who still doubted) I said, "When Ronald and I stand before our Maker, we stand on the same ground. We are both saved by the same Redeemer and by the same "AMAZING GRACE". Many of those present expressed their thanks and appreciation for those re-assuring words.

"All is of grace" is a motto we must not and dare not forget. If Ronald was here, he would own every word of this beautiful old hymn:

> *"Jesus paid it all;*
> *All to him I owe;*
> *Sin had left a crimson stain,*
> *He washed it white as snow!"*

EPILOGUE: I have for a long time wanted to write a book primarily to encourage Seminary students and young pastors who are dealing with discouragement, weariness and who are likely heading for 'burn out'.

I often felt God's nudge/promptings to write but never got down to doing it. I thought I would wait for retirement at which time I would have lots of time to write, but unfortunately, it didn't happen that way.

I must thank all who pushed (and kept on pushing) me to write this book: too many to mention. Of particular mention is my son Graeme, who told me to write the book even if he was the only one who would read it. One day he purchased a Manuscript book, gave it to me and said, "Here, write!"

Thanks to all who prayed, stood by my side and supported me over the years and those who ministered to me (without whom this story could never have been written).

Thanks also to those who so lovingly and willingly helped me with the script (editing and in many other ways) – Chris and Joan Pullenayegem , my son Graeme, my daughter Nicola and my wife Lorraine.

The title and theme of this book is "The Light Shines Through". I hope you were enlightened and encouraged by its contents through the Word and Spirit of God.

Dear reader, my prayer is that the same Light will shine on you, too – turning your darkness (or dark moments) into God's marvelous, liberating light, in and through the Lord Jesus Christ (who IS the Light). Remember the song, "It is no secret what God can do".